This Notebook Belongs To

Mo Tu We Th Fr Sa Su

Top Priorities

Things To Do

Top Priorities

Mo Tu We Th Fr Sa Su

Things To Do

Top Priorities

Mo Tu We Th Fr Sa Su

Things To Do

Top Priorities

Mo Tu We Th Fr Sa Su

Things To Do

Top Priorities

Date : ___________________________

Mo	Tu	We	Th	Fr	Sa	Su
◯	◯	◯	◯	◯	◯	◯

Things To Do

Top Priorities

Date : ___________________________

Mo	Tu	We	Th	Fr	Sa	Su

Things To Do

Top Priorities

Date : ___________________________

Mo Tu We Th Fr Sa Su

Things To Do

Date : ___________________________________

Mo Tu We Th Fr Sa Su

Top Priorities

Things To Do

Top Priorities

Things To Do

Top Priorities

Things To Do

Top Priorities

Mo	Tu	We	Th	Fr	Sa	Su

Things To Do

Top Priorities

Date : _______________

Mo Tu We Th Fr Sa Su

Things To Do

Top Priorities

Date : ______________________

Mo Tu We Th Fr Sa Su

Things To Do

Top Priorities

Things To Do

Top Priorities

Mo Tu We Th Fr Sa Su

Things To Do

Top Priorities

Date : ______________________

Mo	Tu	We	Th	Fr	Sa	Su
◯	◯	◯	◯	◯	◯	◯

Things To Do

Top Priorities

Things To Do

Top Priorities

Date : __________________

Mo Tu We Th Fr Sa Su

Things To Do

Top Priorities

Mo	Tu	We	Th	Fr	Sa	Su

Things To Do

Top Priorities

Date : ______________________

Mo Tu We Th Fr Sa Su

Things To Do

Top Priorities

Things To Do

Top Priorities

Date : __________________________

| Mo | Tu | We | Th | Fr | Sa | Su |

○
○
○

Things To Do

○
○
○
○
○
○
○
○
○
○
○
○
○
○
○

Top Priorities

Things To Do

Top Priorities

Mo Tu We Th Fr Sa Su

Things To Do

Top Priorities

Date : ________________

Mo	Tu	We	Th	Fr	Sa	Su
○	○	○	○	○	○	○

Things To Do

Top Priorities

Mo Tu We Th Fr Sa Su

Things To Do

Top Priorities

Things To Do

Top Priorities

Date : ___________________________

Mo	Tu	We	Th	Fr	Sa	Su
◯	◯	◯	◯	◯	◯	◯

- ◯ ___________________________
- ◯ ___________________________
- ◯ ___________________________

Things To Do

- ◯ ___________________________
- ◯ ___________________________
- ◯ ___________________________
- ◯ ___________________________
- ◯ ___________________________
- ◯ ___________________________
- ◯ ___________________________
- ◯ ___________________________
- ◯ ___________________________
- ◯ ___________________________
- ◯ ___________________________
- ◯ ___________________________
- ◯ ___________________________
- ◯ ___________________________
- ◯ ___________________________

Top Priorities

Things To Do

Top Priorities

Date : _______________________

Mo	Tu	We	Th	Fr	Sa	Su

Things To Do

Top Priorities

Date : __________________

Mo Tu We Th Fr Sa Su

Things To Do

Top Priorities

Date : _______________________

Mo Tu We Th Fr Sa Su

Things To Do

Top Priorities

Mo   Tu   We   Th   Fr   Sa   Su

Things To Do

Top Priorities

Things To Do

Top Priorities

Date : ___________________

Mo	Tu	We	Th	Fr	Sa	Su
○	○	○	○	○	○	○

Things To Do

Date : _______________________________

Mo   Tu   We   Th   Fr   Sa   Su
○   ○   ○   ○   ○   ○   ○

Top Priorities

○ _______________________________
○ _______________________________
○ _______________________________

Things To Do

○ _______________________________
○ _______________________________
○ _______________________________
○ _______________________________
○ _______________________________
○ _______________________________
○ _______________________________
○ _______________________________
○ _______________________________
○ _______________________________
○ _______________________________
○ _______________________________
○ _______________________________
○ _______________________________
○ _______________________________

Mo Tu We Th Fr Sa Su

Top Priorities

Things To Do

Top Priorities

Date : _______________

Mo	Tu	We	Th	Fr	Sa	Su
◯	◯	◯	◯	◯	◯	◯

Things To Do

Top Priorities

Date : _______________

Mo Tu We Th Fr Sa Su

Things To Do

Top Priorities

Date : ________________________

Mo	Tu	We	Th	Fr	Sa	Su
◯	◯	◯	◯	◯	◯	◯

Things To Do

Top Priorities

Date : _______________________

Mo Tu We Th Fr Sa Su

Things To Do

Top Priorities

Date : _______________

Mo Tu We Th Fr Sa Su

Things To Do

Top Priorities

Things To Do

Top Priorities

Things To Do

Top Priorities

Date : ______________

Mo	Tu	We	Th	Fr	Sa	Su
○	○	○	○	○	○	○

Things To Do

Top Priorities

Date : _______________

Mo Tu We Th Fr Sa Su

Things To Do

Top Priorities

Mo Tu We Th Fr Sa Su

Things To Do

Top Priorities

Date : ___________________________

Mo	Tu	We	Th	Fr	Sa	Su
◯	◯	◯	◯	◯	◯	◯

Things To Do

Top Priorities

Things To Do

Top Priorities

Things To Do

Top Priorities

Date : _______________

Mo Tu We Th Fr Sa Su

Things To Do

Top Priorities

Mo Tu We Th Fr Sa Su

Things To Do

Top Priorities

Things To Do

Top Priorities

Things To Do

Top Priorities

Things To Do

Top Priorities

Things To Do

Top Priorities

Mo Tu We Th Fr Sa Su

Things To Do

Top Priorities

Date : ______________

Mo	Tu	We	Th	Fr	Sa	Su
◯	◯	◯	◯	◯	◯	◯

Things To Do

Top Priorities

Things To Do

Top Priorities

Things To Do

Top Priorities

Things To Do

Top Priorities

Date : __________________

Mo Tu We Th Fr Sa Su

Things To Do

Top Priorities

Date : ___________________________

Mo Tu We Th Fr Sa Su

Things To Do

Top Priorities

| Mo | Tu | We | Th | Fr | Sa | Su |

Things To Do

Top Priorities

Things To Do

Top Priorities

Date : ________________

| Mo | Tu | We | Th | Fr | Sa | Su |

Things To Do

Top Priorities

Things To Do

Top Priorities

Mo Tu We Th Fr Sa Su

Things To Do

Top Priorities

Mo Tu We Th Fr Sa Su

Things To Do

Top Priorities

Date : ___________

Mo	Tu	We	Th	Fr	Sa	Su
○	○	○	○	○	○	○

Things To Do

Top Priorities

Date : ___________________

Mo	Tu	We	Th	Fr	Sa	Su

Things To Do

Top Priorities

Things To Do

Top Priorities

Date : __________________________

Mo   Tu   We   Th   Fr   Sa   Su

○ ______________________________
○ ______________________________
○ ______________________________

Things To Do

○ ______________________________
○ ______________________________
○ ______________________________
○ ______________________________
○ ______________________________
○ ______________________________
○ ______________________________
○ ______________________________
○ ______________________________
○ ______________________________
○ ______________________________
○ ______________________________
○ ______________________________
○ ______________________________
○ ______________________________

Top Priorities

Date : _______________

Mo Tu We Th Fr Sa Su

Things To Do

Top Priorities

Mo Tu We Th Fr Sa Su

Things To Do

Top Priorities

Date : ________________

Mo Tu We Th Fr Sa Su

Things To Do

Top Priorities

Things To Do

Top Priorities

Mo   Tu   We   Th   Fr   Sa   Su

Things To Do

Top Priorities

Date : ________________________

Mo	Tu	We	Th	Fr	Sa	Su
○	○	○	○	○	○	○

Things To Do

Top Priorities

Date : _______________

Mo Tu We Th Fr Sa Su

Things To Do

Top Priorities

Things To Do

Top Priorities

Things To Do

Top Priorities

Date : _______________

Mo Tu We Th Fr Sa Su

Things To Do

Top Priorities

Things To Do

Top Priorities

Mo Tu We Th Fr Sa Su

Things To Do

Top Priorities

Date : ___________________

Mo	Tu	We	Th	Fr	Sa	Su
◯	◯	◯	◯	◯	◯	◯

Things To Do

Top Priorities

Mo Tu We Th Fr Sa Su

Things To Do

Top Priorities

Things To Do

Top Priorities

Things To Do

Date : _______________________

Mo Tu We Th Fr Sa Su

Top Priorities

Things To Do

Top Priorities

Things To Do

Top Priorities

Date : _______________

Mo	Tu	We	Th	Fr	Sa	Su
◯	◯	◯	◯	◯	◯	◯

Things To Do

Top Priorities

Things To Do

Top Priorities

Things To Do

Top Priorities

Things To Do

Top Priorities

Things To Do

Top Priorities

Date : _______________

Mo Tu We Th Fr Sa Su

Things To Do

Top Priorities

Things To Do

Top Priorities

| Mo | Tu | We | Th | Fr | Sa | Su |

Things To Do

Top Priorities

Things To Do

Top Priorities

Date : ______________________

| Mo | Tu | We | Th | Fr | Sa | Su |

Things To Do

Top Priorities

Mo Tu We Th Fr Sa Su

Things To Do

Top Priorities

Date : ________________________

Mo	Tu	We	Th	Fr	Sa	Su
○	○	○	○	○	○	○

Things To Do

Top Priorities

Date : _______________

Mo	Tu	We	Th	Fr	Sa	Su
◯	◯	◯	◯	◯	◯	◯

Things To Do

Top Priorities

Mo Tu We Th Fr Sa Su

Things To Do

Top Priorities

Date : _______________

Mo Tu We Th Fr Sa Su

Things To Do

Top Priorities

Date : ________________________

| Mo | Tu | We | Th | Fr | Sa | Su |

Things To Do

Top Priorities

Date : ___________

	Mo	Tu	We	Th	Fr	Sa	Su
	○	○	○	○	○	○	○

Things To Do

Top Priorities

Date : ________________________

Mo	Tu	We	Th	Fr	Sa	Su
○	○	○	○	○	○	○

Things To Do